I0214721

Raising Thoughtful Children Without Going Crazy!

From The Perspective of a Mom and Educator

Corinne Forman, M.Ed

Jones Media Publishing

Raising Thoughtful Children Without Going Crazy!:
From The Perspective of a Mom and Educator

Copyright © 2023 by Corinne B. Forman

All rights reserved. No part of this publication may be reproduced, distributed, or transmitted in any form or by any means, including photocopying, recording, or other electronic or mechanical methods, without the prior written permission of the author, except in the case of brief quotations embodied in critical reviews and certain other noncommercial uses permitted by copyright law.

Jones Media Publishing
10645 N. Tatum Blvd. Ste. 200-166
Phoenix, AZ 85028
www.JonesMediaPublishing.com

Disclaimer:
The author strives to be as accurate and complete as possible in the creation of this book, notwithstanding the fact that the author does not warrant or represent at any time that the contents within are accurate due to the rapidly changing nature of the Internet.

While all attempts have been made to verify information provided in this publication, the Author and the Publisher assume no responsibility and are not liable for errors, omissions, or contrary interpretation of the subject matter herein. The Author and Publisher hereby disclaim any liability, loss or damage incurred as a result of the application and utilization, whether directly or indirectly, of any information, suggestion, advice, or procedure in this book. Any perceived slights of specific persons, peoples, or organizations are unintentional.

In practical advice books, like anything else in life, there are no guarantees of income made. Readers are cautioned to rely on their own judgment about their individual circumstances to act accordingly. Readers are responsible for their own actions, choices, and results. This book is not intended for use as a source of legal, business, accounting or financial advice. All readers are advised to seek the services of competent professionals in legal, business, accounting, and finance field.

Printed in the United States of America

ISBN: 978-1-948382-63-2 paperback

This book is dedicated to my loving family. Fortunate to have built a life enriched with love and support from my husband and children, I thank them for fulfilling me and motivating me to be the best person I can be. Raising my children with my husband has taught me valuable life lessons which I hope to share with you.

As an educator, my students, colleagues, and support staff have enabled me to be a better teacher, colleague, mentor, and administrator. They have provided me with the never-ending work that is needed to raise thoughtful, intelligent, caring, smart, and devoted students. The lessons I've learned are those I try to instill in both my students and my own children.

I am grateful for all those I have interfaced with professionally and personally. It is with all these experiences and relationships that compelled me to write this book. I hope you find it useful.

TABLE OF CONTENTS

PREFACE

The moment a child enters the world, parents ask, "Now what?" This book helps answer that question. The journey of raising thoughtful children feels long at times but it is worth every moment. Instilling core values that promote well-rounded and productive people is the desired end result of this journey. As a parent of teenagers and an educator for over 25 years, my experiences might assist other families with their own adventures in raising children. With this book, I assure you there are helpful takeaways you can implement with your own children beginning today.

As of the publication of this book, I have an 18-year-old daughter attending her last year of high school, working part-time, and maneuvering through the process of entering college. My 16-year-old son is now driving, showing more independence, while navigating through honor's classes with high ambitions for his future. My children are thoughtful people, yet have their own struggles, just like their parents.

Raising my children and having taught countless students, I have learned the following lessons:

- Be present for your children.
- Promote healthy habits/routines.
- Incorporate family time.
- Ask questions without judgment.
- Use humor appropriately.
- Truly listen to your children.
- Let children lead conversations.
- Compromise, rather than say "No."
- Create flexible boundaries.
- Appreciate every moment.

It doesn't matter how old your children are; these lessons are appropriate at any age. Even as adults, we desire to feel heard, validated, and appreciated. These are the elements our children require to feel valued. In *Psychology Today* (2017), "The Psychology Behind Success and Failure," Renée Fabian writes:

> We all want the same thing: simply to be valued by somebody else. Think about every person you have ever met. They just want to feel valued. I want to feel valued, and so do you. By someone.

Our children need to feel valued otherwise they struggle immensely. I believe that, if not found within their own family, children will look to the "outside" to feel that sense of belonging. Therefore, I've done my best to ensure that my family remains a strong, loving "family unit." Without any one of us, the family unit would be truly fragmented. Therefore, both of my children know how much they are valued and appreciated. They know, without a doubt, their parents will always be there for them during their best moments as well as the more difficult ones. They know I will go to great lengths to support them and do my best to not fail them. Because of this, my children have sought friendships with those who are healthy, positive influences, rather than seeking detrimental relationships.

As Dr. Haim G. Ginott wrote in in book, *Between Parent and Child,* 1965:

> When children feel understood, their loneliness and hurt diminish. When children are understood, their love for the parent is deepened. A parent's sympathy serves as emotional first aid for bruised feelings.
>
> When we genuinely acknowledge a child's plight and voice her disappointment, she often gathers the strength to face reality (p. 8).

Relationship Fulfillment

It's critical for children's psyches to truly know and fully understand that – *no matter what poor decisions they make or predicaments they encounter* – a parent will always be there for them. Knowing and trusting that you will be there for them, no matter what, allows them the space and comfort to explore, make their own mistakes, and handle the consequences. This is critical for their growth and maturity.

As a former English teacher, I've seen firsthand how the relationships students have with their families can impact their friendships and behavior in school. For those who feel a sense of belonging at home, I've seen healthy relationships with their peers and teachers. For those less engaged at home, I find greater struggles, some even expressing familial and internal conflict in their school papers. It's important for teachers to nurture their students by supporting them, listening to them, and connecting with them and their families.

A student once wrote to me stating that, through my understanding of her words and my responses to her narrative essays, she gained the courage to move forward and embrace life. She had felt lonely and abandoned at home; she did not receive the adequate love and support she so deserved. By receiving understanding and assurance from her teacher, she started to develop a sense of importance and belonging. It's easy for students like her to fall into bad habits and hang out with "the wrong crowd," simply for any sense of belonging. I was glad to provide her with the tools and encouragement she needed to succeed. Remember, if kids don't receive support at home, they will search for it elsewhere.

I had other students who wrote of parents who encouraged them, inspired them, and desired for them to seek help with any challenges they faced. Through their writings, it became clear there was a correlation between the students who had strong support systems at home and their performance both in and outside of school and those who did not. By having a well-grounded foundation, these students know they'll be assisted and acknowledged along the way as they work toward their goals and dreams. It's important for parents to recognize this and to work at building a solid ground to raise strong children.

Unfortunately, I have also witnessed students make detrimental decisions to their livelihood. As their teacher, I saw them struggle with wanting to do well but feeling defeated. Their desire to feel included in a peer group superseded any academic ambitions they may have had. I believe this longing stemmed from a lack of happiness at home. I read many narrative essays that spoke to feelings of loneliness, not feeling valued, and no sense of belonging; all of this, in turn, can lead to decreased self-worth.

It is crucial that families band together and support each other. Children must feel appreciated and important. There are simple steps guardians can take to create a loving and supporting atmosphere.

This book will provide you with the essentials your children need to successfully move through their schooling years. My hope, as both a parent and an educator, is that my experiences will help to guide you on your own journey.

CHAPTER 1

FAMILY VALUES

Every generation faces new challenges, setting them apart from those who came before. With constant technological advances and information available 24/7, our children's experiences change *daily*. As parents, it's difficult to "keep up" with all of the constant changes, but it's critical to adapt in an effort to maintain a strong core and family foundation. It can be overwhelming, however, that's why it's so important to implement family values. This way, no matter what societal changes occur, you and your children still know what's truly important at the end of the day. Strong values serve as guidelines for living; values aid in knowing what's acceptable and what's not. Though they may not always act like it, the truth is, children of all ages crave parental approval and seek guidelines to help them make honorable decisions.

The Necessity of Positive Communication

According to Dr. Haim G. Ginott, author of *Between Parent and Child*, empathetic conversations allow children to learn and understand the differences between right and wrong; this puts them on a positive path to maintain their integrity and values. Not only is it important for parents to lead by example and to model well-intentioned actions, it's just as important to handle consequences with grace if things don't manifest as planned. Children are astute observers, watching all that we do. It's essential for them to witness all aspects of compromises and negotiation to comprehend the depth of decisions and repercussions. Dr. Ginott states:

> An empathic response that mirrors to children their upset feelings and expresses the parents' sympathy and understanding is effective in changing children's angry moods (p. 55).

The key is to maintain an open and honest communication policy with your children. Discussing matters calmly and thoughtfully allows for reflections and alternate ways of seeking solutions. Dr. Ginott continues to write:

> Communication with children should be based on respect and on skill; it requires (a) that messages preserve the child's as well as the parent's self-respect; and (b) that statements of understanding precede statements of advice or instruction (p. 12).

Teachable Moments

There are so many lessons to be learned outside of school. It's important for parents to share issues that arise at work and in relationships. Simply teach what you know without overthinking it; from pitching a tent, fishing, and plumbing to astronomy, cooking, business and more, all of these fields and hobbies are important. Let your children witness how you handle differences of opinions in appropriate ways and solve issues that transpire. You are their greatest role model! These lessons, along with school-based instruction, are crucial to raising well-rounded children.

My husband is an entrepreneur and has a strong understanding of business and finances. Ever since our children were young, we've provided age-appropriate lessons on developing business ideas and financial awareness. As they grew older, conversations shifted to the stock market and career aspirations. We even created contests to keep our children engaged; we'd all pick different stocks we thought would do well and followed the stock market to see which ones thrived the most. While these conversations were frequent, we made sure they weren't overwhelming. In fact, our children often approached us with ideas and questions, which my husband and I relished and used as teachable moments. Be sure to seize the opportunities that fall into your lap and assist your children in thinking "big." Let them know there are so many opportunities for them and provide as many engaging experiences for them as possible.

CNBC contributor and author Margot Machol Bisnow wrote a 2022 article about raising successful kids. She writes:

> As parents, we all want to raise confident, fearless and resilient kids. But where do we begin?

For my book, *Raising an Entrepreneur,* I talked to 70 parents who raised highly successful people. When I asked them what skills they taught their kids at an early age, there was one in particular that they all agreed on: curiosity.

Curiosity goes further than a simple desire to know something. It involves trying to fix something. It's about asking questions: How does this work? Does it have to be this way? Could I make it better?

Margot lists three important factors to accomplish increasing kids' curiosity. They include: (1) encourage kids to fix things, (2) instill confidence to tackle big, real-world problems, and (3) ask hard questions.

She further explains:

1. Fixing things can help kids develop decision-making and problem-solving skills. If you have something around the house that needs repairing, like a bad light bulb or leaky faucet, use it as a teaching opportunity with your kids. It's also okay to admit if you're unsure how to fix something. Knowing where to *find* accurate information is just as important as knowing it from the start.

2. Sharing a mother-daughter quote: "We were always learning things together, playing games, exploring or having little adventures. This spirit prepared me to be an entrepreneur — to be proactive and see opportunities in the world."

3. Smart questions show that you respect your kid's judgment, which builds their confidence. It also teaches them how to manage risk and how to make choices among different possibilities with various trade-offs and different outcomes.

When teaching my 7th grade students how to write an explanatory essay for which they had to learn a new task and explain it thoroughly, one particular student chose to learn how to change a flat tire. She thought it would be easy to learn and write about as her father was a mechanic. However, she found herself struggling with the process on her own. With the support from her father, who provided patience, repetition, and modeling, she not only learned how to change a flat tire, she wrote a masterpiece essay to boot. This is just one example of how vital it is for parents and educators to join forces and teach our students necessary life skills. It makes for a richer and more independent life.

Additionally, it's critical to model *responsibility*. Children must learn how to be responsible for their belongings, their work, and their actions within their relationships (family, friends, future colleagues, bosses, etc.). Caring for pets, tending to a garden, washing cars, cleaning the house, and making a bed are all examples of role modeling responsibility.

Please recognize the difference between teaching *chores* and *manners*. Chores are a great way to teach children responsibility as they contribute to overall household needs. While some families view chores as jobs that merit payment, others may see chores as an expected family contribution; it's up to your family to decide what makes the most sense.

Now, teaching manners is a very separate task and is best done through modeling day in and day out. Manners cannot be enforced, nor can they be taught. Research has shown that modeling the behavior you deem *important* is the ultimate way to teach. Again, this all goes back to what you value most and what you want your children to emulate as they grow into adults. Dr. Ginott discusses it in his book:

> Children's inner emotional reaction to our instruction is a decisive element in how much they learn of what we want them to know. Values cannot be taught directly. They are absorbed, and become part of the child, only through identification with, and emulation of, persons who gain his or her love and respect (p. 77-78).

Teaching by Modeling

I wanted to teach my son to be thoughtful and considerate with other people. Rather than *tell* him what I wanted him to do, I modeled the behavior myself. I began by holding doors open for him and waiting to eat until he was at the table. I also made a point to share with him what I was doing and why. I wasn't yelling at him or coaching him; I was simply teaching by doing and through bits of wisdom and small talk. Valuable lessons were learned and he has become a wonderful and caring 16-year-old boy.

I had another student who lost his dad at an early age, but was raised by an extraordinary mom. His mom was respectful, kind, and giving. She showed incredible interest in his academics and in his entire life. She taught him manners and how to be kind to others, even strangers. She modeled this in an exemplary fashion. This boy was in many honors' classes, including my honors English Language Arts class. He competed and excelled in dance classes and contests, helped special needs students at school, and had many friends as he was known to be kind-hearted, caring, and smart. I remember hoping my son would emulate these behaviors. After asking his mother how she'd raised such an incredible child, she said she modeled the behaviors she desired and then praised her son when she noticed him practicing the same behaviors. It really can be that easy!

Of course, a parent's job is never really over; it grows and evolves as our children age. But it's easier when strong values are instilled from a young age. And it's important to relish each moment, big and small, to show your children how much you value them. Giving praise is a great way to be both thoughtful and constructive with children. It is critical to praise their *efforts and accomplishments; as* Dr. Ginott writes:

> The single most important rule is that praise deals only with children's efforts and accomplishments, not with their character and personality (p. 32).
>
> Our words should state clearly what we like and appreciate about their effort, help, work, consideration, creation, or accomplishments...... Our words should be like a magic canvas upon which children cannot help but paint a positive picture of themselves (p. 34).

Dr. Ginott continues stating that helping our children through guidance *rather than criticism* is much more beneficial. Criticism attacks personality traits, whereas guidance assists in finding solutions (p. 39).

When praising my children's efforts on working on homework, studying for tests, washing the windows, or cleaning the dishes, I've found that they tend to do more of those tasks, unprompted. I once had a student who would arrive to class each day looking rather glum. He'd consistently ask for extra credit as he struggled with grammar assignments. He would come to my classroom for additional hours, telling me his parents were disappointed with him, even though he studied every day. I told him how proud I was of him for his effort, and I continued to work with him. Once he understood the content, he still continued to attend my office hours. When I asked him about it, he told me he felt happy knowing I was proud of the effort he was making, as he wasn't receiving that at home.

Sometimes, it's not about the end goal; the high grades, landing the spot on the varsity team, etc. It's simply about the effort you make. It's so important to recognize and highlight this in your children; do you really care if they get straight "As" in every single subject? Or do you value the fact that they're putting forth the effort? Eventually, the results will come, but the process of getting there is what builds character and work ethic, and that should absolutely be recognized.

Valuable Parenting Tips

1. Spend quality time each day, even for just ten minutes, with your children.

2. Share your own struggles while modeling ways to resolve them.

3. Be involved with your child's schooling and friendships.

4. From an educator's perspective, provide opportunities for students to share their thoughts and experiences with you via meaningful projects

and assignments. Students crave a listening audience.

5. Be mindful when communicating with your children.

6. Ask questions and provide an empathetic ear.

7. Only suggest ideas if your child desires.

8. Create opportunities for your children to learn life skills and responsibility.

9. Listen, listen, listen.

10. Rephrase what you are hearing your children say to ensure you are understanding correctly.

CHAPTER 2

BALANCED LIFESTYLE

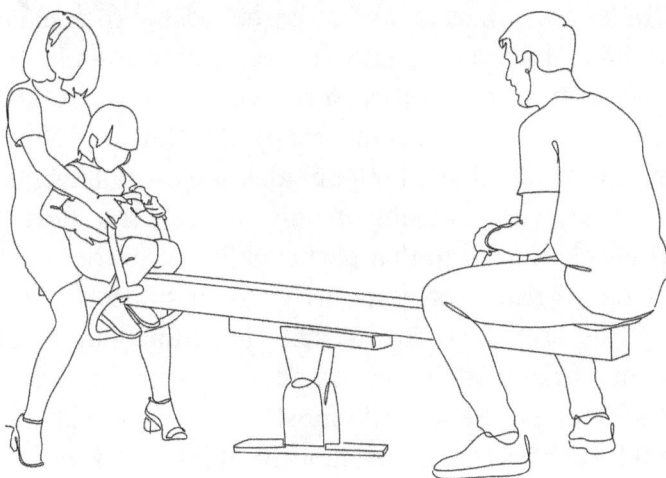

Life is all about balance. From work and relationships to health and fitness, navigating everything can prove to be quite the juggling act. It's easier for adults to take a step back and realize when more balance may be necessary. However, kids are often steeped in schoolwork and faced with pressures (from both their parents and teachers) to achieve academic greatness when, in reality, that's not the end-all and be-all.

Process v. Final Product

Grades are important and no parent wishes their child to fail. However, greater concentration should be placed on effort. In other words, goals change, but the process doesn't. We know strong study skills and effort will help one achieve better grades and overall results; however, when focusing on only one task, the effort is solely channeled to that particular event, rather than used for various interests, activities, or subjects.

Research has shown that the effort put forth from students is the outcome teachers prefer to see. Students will benefit the most when encouraged to put forth effort both at school and at home. Of course, the key to this is finding a balance.

Think back to being a school-aged kid yourself; what were your primary concerns and struggles? Did you ever feel overwhelmed, unsupported, or off-balance? This goes back to what your family values most. If a child feels that top grades are all that matter, it can lead to a lot of pressure and stress. However, if it's clear that the value is placed on the effort that is made, well, that can make things a bit easier.

This, of course, doesn't mean we shouldn't care to understand a student's discrepancy between understanding of the material yet not demonstrating the knowledge on assignments. Communication with our children and their teachers is *necessary*. Supporting our children with extra help, such as hiring tutors and attending teacher conferences, is non-negotiable. This exploration is an attempt to assist our children in learning better study strategies and finding a better balance to work through it all.

In *Psychology Today*, Ms. Fabian writes about having a "Growth Mindset:"

> How we view and manage failure helps cultivate success in our lives, and that starts with having a growth mindset. A growth mindset means that we believe through hard work and effort we can grow and learn, even in the face of failure. It means we believe mastery is possible if we keep trying, keep taking chances, and work toward improving. Failure is not a permanent condition.

> "When we believe that abilities are fixed (fixed mindset), we interpret failure as evidence for the lack of ability, and we stop trying," writes Louai Rahal, based on psychologist Carol Dweck's work. "When we believe that abilities can be stretched with learning (growth mindset), we perceive failures

as opportunities for learning and we reflect on failures in order to stretch our abilities."

During his freshman year of high school, my son took a biology class in which he studied vigorously for every quiz and test and always completed his homework on time. Even with all of his effort, he barely earned a "C" in the class. Frustrated and confused, he turned to the school for some guidance and learned that different study methods and tools would be more beneficial for this particular course. After implementing these new methods, his grades improved.

Moments like this are essential for our children's development. Giving up is not the answer but, rather, we should seek new and improved solutions to achieve our goals. I was proud of my son for recognizing this and making the effort to do better. This process is paramount in everyday living. We all must learn how to persevere through troubled moments and successful times.

Interestingly, I recall former students who performed poorly on tests as they struggled to grasp certain content; meanwhile, others who simply guessed correctly or understood the content easily earned better grades. Years later, I'd run into my former students or their parents as I was out and about; I learned that those who struggled found alternative methods to help them thrive. Conversely, those who did well without much effort actually had a more difficult time in college and in the workforce.

These students had to learn better methods to succeed in life. This underscores the point of mastering the *process* is key. This is a valuable lesson!

Physical and Social Play

While school is a priority, especially for children, health, safety, and a balanced lifestyle supersedes it. It is important to have a strong sense of how to live a balanced, healthy lifestyle. Parents modeling work ethic, morality, and a range of interests is essential.

In a *Children's Hospital of Philadelphia's* article, "The Benefits of Outdoor Play: Why it Matters," the necessity of *active play time* is highlighted. All children and adults need regular exercise. It helps them stay healthy, sleep well, and incur stable functionality. The article states:

> Outdoor play is beneficial for children beyond the physical activity it provides. It helps them socialize, understand their bodies better, engage in imaginative play and enjoy the outdoors. In today's busy and complex world, it can be difficult to schedule outdoor time with your child. But, it is something you should prioritize for your child's healthy growth and development.

> School-aged children need about three hours of outdoor play each day. While this is a lot to add to a daily schedule, the activity will contribute to the physical and emotional health of your child.

Outdoor time and unstructured play is even more beneficial for young children. This incorporates playing at the park or play dates. The article continues to detail:

> Unstructured physical activity improves the health of your child. It reduces the likelihood of obesity and weight-related health concerns which are becoming bigger issues for families today. Outdoor play also improves mental health as a result of physical activity.

Think about your own work/life balance. *When you feel stressed out, what do you do?* Perhaps, you grab a coffee, read a book, or take a walk. Even just a ten-minute break can be incredibly beneficial, giving you the clarity you need to move forward. The same should be applied to the needs of your children. While school is a primary focus in their younger years, it shouldn't be everything. Encourage them to take breaks, get outside, and play for a bit! Encourage the BALANCE!

Flexible Boundaries

Technology plays a huge role in our children's lives both in and out of school. As parents and educators, we should encourage breaks from devices; of course, this is best demonstrated through modeling this behavior ourselves. Dr. Katie K. Lockwood encourages this by saying,

> It promotes active engagement with their peers and the natural environment, and helps them develop respect for the world and consideration for others around them. Replacing some recreational screen time with outdoor play also helps reduce the risks of a sedentary lifestyle.

Not only that, but being active also improves a person's sleep, mood, and overall social skills. "Outdoor play helps children grow socially, helping them to develop healthy ways of forming friendships, responding to physical interaction, and using their imaginations to entertain each other," says Dr. Lockwood. "It helps them solve problems, build relationships within their peer group and gain a respect for nature."

To allow for a balanced lifestyle, *flexible* boundaries must be in place. Again, reflect on your own life as an adult; not every situation or circumstance is the same. You need to be able to conform at times to maintain balance. Of course, boundaries are put in place to ensure your child's safety. Most often we see boundaries set for curfews, dates, social events, etc. When we see children who dismiss boundaries, cross lines, and break rules, it's often due to a lack of trust, communication, understanding, and/or flexibility.

Therefore, creating situational understanding is critical to maintaining communication and honesty. Again, as parents, we must implement understanding to build trust in our relationships with our children. It's not just about parents trusting their children; our children must trust us as well.

Having flexible boundaries also means supporting our children's interests and balancing the importance of those interests with family, friendships, and schoolwork. Consistently discussing upcoming events in conjunction with schoolwork is necessary. Create a verbal game plan daily or weekly to ensure all tasks and expectations are met. Of course, there will be days when it feels like there are just too many hours to burn and other days where it seems there just isn't enough time. By having your priorities straight and a schedule in place, the week allows for more peaceful (non-argumentative) moments. *And the bonus?* Everything gets accomplished!

Flexible Boundaries while Embracing Technology

According to Dr. Russell's article in *They Are The Future: Flexible Parenting and Boundaries,*

> We have all heard about the "dangers" of technology being reported in the media. Without a doubt, many hours each day spent on electronic devices could impact a child in many ways:

- Takes away from opportunities for face-to-face social contact and practicing friendship skills.

- Takes away from time which could be spent engaging in physical activity.

- Research studies show that the short-term "buzzes"/rewards provided by computer games and social media actually change the way the brain works; in particular, the dopamine reward system in the brain changes. This means the child increasingly seeks short-term buzzes and is less able to wait for rewards.

On the flip side, some computer games do teach valuable skills. Apps and games can allow introverted teenagers to meet and engage with others in the cyber world, giving them a way to practice their social skills.

Instilling Well-Roundedness

Every parent wants well-rounded children, as we're quick to boast to our friends and family when our children not only achieve high grades but do it all while also involved in many clubs and activities. *But do you ever consider how taxing this lifestyle can be to a child?*

So, why put our children through this? This is a tough predicament. Parents want their children to be involved in activities and to do well in school.

We want them to not only be active, but to have an engaging social life too. This parental pressure, in turn, puts pressure on our children. But it's on us to recognize which pressures are coming from society and which are coming from inside our own homes.

For my family, our priority is to ensure our children are involved with physical, mental, or musical activities along with their schoolwork. They can partake in "extra activities," so long as they uphold their grades. However, we are not stringent on straight "As." We just want our children to feel success in school and in the activities they participate in. With that said, I don't wish failure upon either of my children but there is much research to say that failure builds character, perseverance, and knowledge. These are exactly the traits I wish to bestow upon them! *The Psychology Behind Success and Failure* states:

> It turns out that failure is one of humanity's greatest strengths, and therefore is not the opposite of success, but actually a key factor in meeting our goals. This has been proven by evolutionary scientists such as Charles Darwin, who is credited with saying, "It is not the strongest of the species that survives. It is the one that is most adaptable to change."

Many of my students who were involved with school or club sports and activities, were confident, happy, and prepared for school. Those who did not participate in activities lacked self-esteem and seemed less prepared for learning. As a teacher and a parent, I discovered that the more involved students were in activities, the better they managed their time, completed their homework, and felt confident. Those who immediately returned home after school tended to misuse their time.

I recall a group of honor students who would always share with me the details of their club volleyball team tournaments. Their enthusiasm, passion, and excitement was overwhelming. Not only were they delighted to share their victories and losses, but they shared how much work they did on their long car drives to and from tournaments. I'd share these stories with my daughter who was so inspired that she also enrolled for volleyball leagues. Playing team sports had a tremendous impact on her; she found that her true passion was tennis!

The point is, find the excitement your children have for any activity and *embrace* it. Demonstrate a good balance for all things; including responsibilities that may not be so exciting and fun opportunities that align with their passions and values. Let your children discover their own interests; the best thing you can do is to support and encourage the journey, knowing you've instilled good values and modeled great behavior.

While extracurriculars help students to develop solid friendships and feel more motivated overall, there is a flip side. Overextending kids with too many activities can be detrimental. Children should therefore maintain a *balanced* lifestyle. Talk to your children and help them understand that they don't need to be the best of the best at everything. Let them pursue their interests and assist them on their journey. In a *Bricks 4 Kidz* article, "Helping Your Child Explore Their Own Interests," the author writes:

> When children are encouraged to explore their own interests, they will inevitably encounter others who enjoy the same things. Shared interests create a bond between kids. These childhood friendships have profound psychological benefits that can impact a child — both in the short- and long-term.

Importance of Schedules

For those students who study from home through online learning or homeschooling, finding balance is of particular importance. As the Home Instruction Specialist for my district, I found that many students lounged around all day in their beds, on the couch with their cellphones, or watching television. Students need a motivator to become more active with their learning and physical activity. I worked with several families to create a helpful reward system to further motivate students. In fact, one student went from not attending online classes to working five hours a day with breaks and a weekend reward. Again, no matter what the situation is, it's all about creating a *balance*.

Healthy eating habits and exercise are also crucial when it comes to learning proper lifestyle balance. It is not enough to immerse yourself into a variety of activities; one must eat well, exercise, socialize, and maintain healthy academic studying. According to author and clinical psychologist Dr. Brenda Wolfe, eating means following your body's needs. Do not diet and starve yourself, but eat nutritiously to obtain the sustenance your body is craving.

In her book, *A Diet is the Last Thing You Need*, Dr. Wolfe emphasizes the importance of creating a routine to allow for proper daily consumption without over-or undereating. She writes:

> It means structuring your daily routine to minimize the impact of the mismatch between your body and environment, as happens when your body has had enough but the waiter brings out Death-by-Chocolate cake and you eat past comfort (p. 123).

It can be hard for students to find this balance when they're bogged down with school assignments, sports, plays, or whatever else they may be involved in. As their parents, it's your job to demonstrate and encourage healthy habits all around.

To do this, you can prep meals and snacks in advance; better yet, get your child involved with meal prepping! Encourage kids to eat what they need without overeating. On the flipside, you need to encourage your kids to eat even when they have a packed schedule; skipping meals to study or to maintain a certain image is extremely unhealthy. Again, balance is key.

For those who are homeschooled or participate in online learning, increased exercise is critical. Again, creating a routine or schedule is the best way to get out of your chair, off your couch, and away from those glowing screens. To help my children exercise more, I told them to stop while wanting more. For example, start by jogging five minutes a day, even if you want to do more. If they overdo it and burnout, that tends to be the end of it. But, if they stop *before* burnout, they'll be excited to exercise again the next day.

Plus, exercise can be fun! It doesn't have to mean lifting weights or even running for that matter. You can walk, dance, swim, shovel the snow, do a load of laundry (there's some heavy lifting involved there!), and more. If you're up and moving, that's a start. Again, this goes back to family values; do you value being active, and do you demonstrate that through your own actions?

Tips to Maintain Balance

1. Create a weekly or monthly family calendar with all events listed on them. Make it visible for all to see and reference. While a wall calendar is a great visual, you can also utilize a shared calendar on your phone.

2. Teach your children the process of doing something; from study habits and how to write an essay to learning how to cook, anything you are knowledgeable in is helpful to a child's growth.

3. Model and support a balanced lifestyle. Demonstrate a strong work ethic, physical wellness, having a healthy mind, and engaging in activities.

4. Include your children on daily household tasks; even running errands such as grocery shopping, dry cleaning, or washing the car.

5. Include daily physical activity, even if it is short of the suggested medical requirement.

6. Enforce strong study skills.

7. Listen with an empathetic ear.

8. Focus on the process rather than the end result.

9. Ensure health and safety above all else.

10. Provide unstructured play during each day/ week.

CHAPTER 3

SOCIAL MEDIA

Welcome to the age of social media! Whether you like it or not, there's no escaping the buzz of apps and bright, glowing screens that surround us. I found myself, like many other parents, giving my children their first cell phones at an early age. At this point, it's just practical. With busy lifestyles and the loss of landlines, it's the easiest way to stay connected. Of course, there's also the social aspect of having a phone and access to certain apps and programs.

Technology Responsibility

Many school districts have incorporated digital learning programs into their curriculum, so it's important to supplement this learning at home. Of course, we must have a foundation of trust and understanding before gifting children with these technological tools.

It is our responsibility as parents to ensure our children use their phones and computers appropriately. While trying to maintain a trustful, honorable relationship with your children, it is still critical to ensure their safety. After all, research tells us that our brains are not fully formed until our late twenties! *The National Institute of Mental Health* states:

> Though the brain may be done growing in size, it does not finish developing and maturing until the mid- to late 20s. The front part of the brain, called the prefrontal cortex, is one of the last brain regions

to mature. This area is responsible for skills like planning, prioritizing, and controlling impulses. Because these skills are still developing, teens are more likely to engage in risky behaviors without considering the potential results of their decisions.

To assist our children, we need to monitor their online interactions. While I'm not encouraging secretly spying on your children, I am encouraging open conversations about the apps they use, sites they visit, and their thoughts on what they observe through their interactions online. Again, your children will take cues from YOU. *What is your relationship with technology? How often are you on your computer or cellphone?* You can start by discussing the following:

- **Privacy settings:** Investigate what measures you can take to keep content private on the websites you use. On Facebook and other social networking sites, you can adjust your settings so that only the people you select are able to see your personal information and posts. It's important to check these privacy settings frequently because sites sometimes change their policies.

- **Think before you post:** Never forget that the Internet is *public*. What you put out there can never be erased. If you wouldn't say something in a room full of strangers, don't say it via the Internet. Even letting someone know sensitive or embarrassing information about you via email can have unforeseen consequences.

- **Keep personal information personal:** Don't reveal identifying details about yourself—address, phone number, school, credit card number, etc.—online. Passwords exist for a reason; don't share them with friends or strangers.

Pitfalls of Social Media

Social media also brings with it a new form of bullying: *cyberbullying*, which is defined by Merriam-Webster as "the use of electronic communication to bully a person, typically by sending messages of an intimidating or threatening nature." As parents, we must teach our children appropriate online behavior and the ramifications of not embracing it ethically. We also need to supervise, initiate hard conversations, and provide best and worst-case scenarios of sharing information online.

If you're unsure of where to start, the best way to begin is by educating yourself. From there, you can educate others; be sure to involve your children in the conversation and discuss what they can do if they experience cyberbullies.

Providing our children with real-world consequences of any online action, whether positive or negative, is necessary to assist them in understanding consequences of online learning.

Deciding whether or not to listen in on your children's conversations, search their rooms/phones, or question their actions comes with being a parent. Of course, these decisions should be based on your children's personality, responsibility levels, and your relationship with them. This is a *personal* choice that should not be judged, but instead, respected based on your family's needs. Personally, I've found that the more I "checked up" on my children, the more they felt untrusted. As I eased up, our relationships improved. With greater trust between us, my children felt more comfortable confiding in me and thus the need to "check up" was attenuated.

Being both an educator and a mom has caused many internal struggles. I know the "right" thing to do as an educator regarding social media; as a mom, I know the importance of a social life. Educationally, phones must have limits, especially as they are the gateway to social media (the culprit of emotional and physical distraction and mental health issues). According to *Newport Academy*'s article, "The Latest on Teen Cell Phone Addiction,"

> Teenage cell phone addiction goes well beyond texting and talking. It includes apps, games, and, in particular, social media. For teens, cell phones have become a way to comment and criticize, approve and admire. They are not always communicating with friends. Often, they are

commenting on their activities. They are checking for likes and responses to their own posts.

Cell Phone addiction drains our attention. Teens' intense focus on cell phones distracts them. They are not present in their everyday life. Once cell phone addiction sets in, behaviors can change. Grades at school can drop and participation in extracurricular activities can diminish. Did you know that 61 percent of kids say smartphone use has had a negative impact on their schoolwork?

I did not want cell phones to become the cause of mistrust in my household or classroom. It is easy for students to get caught up with peer pressure, especially with social media. Small problems escalate quickly into bigger problems. Therefore, in-depth conversations about cell phone safety and usage must occur and be often.

My children knew that I would not inspect their phones if they continued to be honest with me about using their phones wisely. With that said, kids will be kids and negative experiences did occur over the years; my children sought help and dealt with the repercussions. While some of these situations were difficult and uncomfortable, I did my best to teach my children while assisting them to maneuver through their issues with grace. I believe phone usage and responsibility must be integrated into family conversations regularly.

Although too much of any technology (television, computers, and cell phones) can create negative effects, cell phones are the primary source of socialization. *So, what are we to do?* Obviously, limits must be established and children must understand the consequences of social media – both positive and negative. Digital footprints are an absolute cause for concern in today's society. An embarrassing moment that could once be forgotten about and left to fade as a long-forgotten memory can now go viral and live on forever.

Using Technology Positively

It's important for limits to be placed on social media; from phones and computers to tablets and other forms of internet access. It's easy for even the busiest of students to fall victim to scrolling, posting, and gaming for hours on end. While it can be nice to have a little break in the day, it's not healthy to be glued to a screen. If necessary, create a policy for your kids in which they can "gain" an extra half hour or an hour of screen time when they complete their homework, chores, or something else. Be sure the policies you set make sense for your kids and their schedules/lifestyle, and be flexible!

When teaching students, I found that social media often disrupted the classroom learning environment. Students tended to sneak their phones into class, though their snickers and outbursts were not so secretive. This created a difficult learning environment. In fact, the phone does not even need to be present for students to converse about what they wrote, saw, or read in their social media life.

Educators must learn how to spin social media and technology to their advantage. Rather than dismiss advances in technology altogether, adaptation is key. Assignments and projects should include social media/technology for researching information to learn and think critically. By using technology to learn rather than using it for gossip, students become more engaged and focused.

A student once walked into my classroom, desperately trying to withhold tears. He had been told the day before that he was fat and students had recorded him being teased in the lunchroom. Although this occurred the day prior, the event had been shared across social media all night and morning. The student did not want to attend school, but was forced to.

Both educators and parents need to be aware that our students are constantly affected emotionally which can disrupt learning and their mental health. It is critical to cater to these students and provide them with the care and support necessary to help them cope through the process. This is not to say a teacher cannot continue to instruct, but a little bit of leniency not only helps but also goes a long way in supporting the student's progress moving forward, both academically and emotionally.

Tips for Parenting in the Social Media Age

1. At home, place all cell phones in a central location and set designated times for usage.

2. No technology during meal times.

3. All homework, chores, etc. need to be completed before accessing screens.

4. Discuss digital footprints, especially how it can affect a person's future.

5. Teach ramifications of misuse of social media or online content.

6. Teach appropriate, normal technology behavior and safe searching.

7. Teach appropriate settings to disable others from tracking online usage. I also recommend using these helpful applications across your devices:

<u>Bark</u>: Bark provides parental control over the Internet and across devices. For example, websites can be blocked and monitored. It even detects words or activities that show signs of cyberbullying, depression, inappropriate content, and more.

<u>Net Nanny</u>: Net Nanny allows parents to monitor all digital habits or content and protect them from harmful sites. It also allows parents to limit or control screen time and provide the best safe sites for researching.

Remember, iPhones and Androids also have <u>internal controls</u> to help monitor screen usage. Be sure to review these with your children.

CHAPTER 4

FAMILY TIME

Creating a strong family unit is extremely important, especially in today's modern world. When people try to imagine how to strengthen their families, vacations and travel often come to mind. While exploring the world around is both amazing and educational, family togetherness doesn't have to be that extreme. In fact, it can be as simple as taking walks together in your neighborhood. Other easy examples include at least one daily family meal time, watching a television show or movie together, playing games once or twice a week, going to a show, shopping, or just cuddling on the couch. The point is, every family member should feel connected with one another in some special way throughout the week. Family time shouldn't be put on hold until the next vacation, event, etc. occurs.

Valuing Family Members

We must value each other's time and personal interests while working together to carve out time for one another. During their younger years, our children were regularly involved with sports. Rather than stressing the importance of family dinners, knowing that the kids would be out and about, we enjoyed breakfasts and afternoon snacks together. Sometimes we played board games in the evenings but most time was devoted to playing outside; from bike rides and baseball to tossing a football, playing four square, or basketball; we always ensured some amount of quality time.

Now, with my children in their teenage years, I recognize the importance of more one-on-one time. Whether it be hiking, swimming, walking, taking a trip, or fishing, time spent one-on-one is beneficial for everyone's mental health. According to *Mental Health Center*:

> Family relationships can substantially affect mental health, behavior and even physical health. Numerous studies have shown that social relationships, particularly family relationships, can have both long- and short-term effects on one's mental health. Depending on the nature of these relationships, mental health can be enhanced or impacted negatively.

Quality time with your children is precious; you're creating lifelong memories every time you share a moment together. Time is the most precious commodity we can provide to our loved ones as it is scarce, especially with active families. Therefore, the time we give to each other is more impactful. Simple family time or one-on-one pairing is integral to maintain communication and connections with one another.

Collapsing on my child's bed and taking long strolls have been effective in maintaining an open dialogue and closeness. These moments helped bridge the gap and quell any unease from explosive arguments or misunderstandings. Moments like these allow us to be heard, to share our feelings, and to remember that sometimes you just need to relax and cuddle with your child.

Importance of Family Relationships

In the classroom, I had students who shared with me beautiful moments they spent with their families over the weekend. I also noticed those students who returned to school each Monday seeming sad or lonely. It became clear that many of these students who wrote to me or talked to me before and after school, and during their lunch periods, craved an adult relationship. I kept my door open during lunch to provide these students, and those needing extra help, a place to feel safe and nurtured.

When it comes to nature versus nurture, which one really is more important? Nature definitely has a profound effect on our core; however, nurture is just as valuable. Everyone has a need to feel connected with others and feel a sense of purpose and belonging. While the home is the best environment to receive this, educators must also provide it at school where kids spend the majority of their developmental years.

In fact, this is what the country's founders envisioned in 1867. Although the United States educational system was birthed in 1821, the Department of Education did not exist until 1867. American educator Horace Mann and other reformers worked diligently to provide schooling for all citizens and, in the 1870s, public schools were present state-wide, quickly taking the lead over private and church-based schools. Our school system then transformed to include the three main tiers we know today: elementary, middle, and high school (Brookings).

The focus of schools, according to the *Center on Education Policy* (CEP) in their article, "History and Evolution of Public Education in the US," is to transform children to become moral, productive, and literate adults. To do this, according to the CEP, schools must:

> Teach the "three R's" (reading, writing, arithmetic), along with other subjects such as history, geography, grammar, and rhetoric. A strong dose of moral instruction would also be provided to instill civic virtues.

Of course, the Great Depression affected schools as funding was sparse and teachers lost their jobs. Once society bounced back, schools reopened, but the curriculum shifted. The three R's remained but focused less on factory skills (as technology advanced) and more on leadership skills and social-emotional intelligence. This is critical to recognize, as with the outbreak of COVID-19, our educational system shifted once again. Although we had a setback, it is plausible we can create a better educational system that can withstand future societal outbreaks.

The *Collaborative for Academic, Social, and Emotional Learning* (CASEL), as well as other researchers, are determining the best way to proceed with education in an effort to assist students and families with preventing potential pitfalls. CASEL and others found severe teaching and staff shortages, absenteeism, school closures, social-emotional demand, violence, discipline issues, and ultimately, a loss of quality instruction which has resulted in dropping test scores and the need to implement extra tutoring sessions to assist students. Additionally, online learning has increased, providing more flexibility. While waiting for further plans to assist our students in schools, at home we must do our part. Families must step up and be more active in their children's education.

As children transfer from preschool to elementary, middle, high school, and beyond, their needs change and family dynamics must adjust. Children become influenced by their community of teachers, adult staff, coaches, teammates, peers, peers' families, and more. While the school system has transformed over the years to meet the needs of modern children, it's just as important for parents and families to adapt to the changing times as well. The next chapters offer both parental and educational perspectives to maintain mentally healthy children as they breeze through the next chapters of their lives.

Tips for Cultivating More Family Time

1. Sit on your child's bed and say, "Hi."

2. Ask your child to go on a walk or to assist you in the kitchen, or with chores.

3. Take time each week or day to have a special moment with your family (a meal, game, T.V. show, family walk, etc.).

4. Be flexible with both family and one-on-one activities. Discover new interests together, such as gardening.

5. Secure your family unit.

6. Value all the time you spend together.

7. Value what is felt and said by each member in your family. Cherish the informal, spontaneous moments; they are more valuable than the planned ones!

8. Love each other fully!

CHAPTER 5

ELEMENTARY SCHOOL

Typically serving children in Kindergarten through fifth or sixth grade, elementary school is an interesting time for kids. As each year brings dramatic new growth and changing of interests, it can be difficult for both parents and teachers to keep up. It's also a time when certain learning and environmental issues may start to pop up (it's better to address them early to create healthy patterns moving forward).

From feelings of anxiety, with teachers or friends, feeling alone or lacking a strong social circle, children can easily get caught in a downward spiral. Other issues may include:

- Lack of structure.
- Hyperactivity, cannot focus.
- Slow grasp of understanding material.
- Does not have a good rapport with the main teacher.
- Not feeling valued or appreciated.
- Lonely (i.e. no one to sit with at lunch).
- Lack of fundamental skills in reading and math.
- Not being chosen to join PE or sports' teams.

Catering to Students' Needs

Remember, everyone is born with a variety of abilities, skills, and needs; we're all very different! Some kids are natural athletes, while others are quick-witted debaters. Some may pay attention and still do poorly on tests, while others slack off and still get top grades. While our education system makes it a priority to meet the needs of those children who fall below and above the mainstream, what happens to the average students?

As an educator, I worry most about those students who fall somewhere in the middle. They are not "gifted" nor are they "learning disabled." But these students often need further attention as well.

So, how do we service them? There are various structures we can implement starting *at home.* I recommend creating a family schedule to ensure your children are progressing and obtaining the necessary skills for their future growth and success. It may be time-consuming at first, especially for those parents with full-time jobs of their own, but it's crucial to help propel your kids forward.

As my children entered Kindergarten, I didn't want them to experience schooling the way I did. I did not learn how to organize my homework nor did I ever create a schedule for completing my work. For my generation, schooling was very traditional; it was teacher-focused with not much student engagement. My children's elementary school did a beautiful job teaching organizational skills and maintaining student engagement. I can truly say I was the proud mother of organized children, which helped them to be successful in elementary school.

At Home Support

At home, we reviewed their homework, agenda, books, and conquered any work that had to be finished immediately. We studied for upcoming quizzes and tests. They learned how to organize and structure their workload. We developed creative ways to learn new topics to better assist them with assignments and tests. In fact, these moments were about more than just studying; it connected us in a fun, loving way. Late afternoons were then spent playing sports or attending activities. In the evenings, we'd watch television, dance to music, play board games, or spend time reading.

As years pass, children have new experiences, both positive and negative, that enhance and stifle their growth. Common examples include peer pressure, mental health issues, and struggles with teachers and peers. That's why shared moments at home are so precious. These moments allow us to share our "positives" and "negatives" of the day, further binding us together. This is not to say that if you don't have the time allotted for all of this, that you cannot create a schedule for homework and participate in one activity. One simple activity, like reading before bedtime, is just as precious.

It's important for children to feel safe and supported at home so they can work through any conflict they may be experiencing in school or somewhere else. As a parent, it's also your responsibility to attend teacher meetings and engage in conversations with other parents; in other words, be an *active participant* in your child's life. School is about so much more than academic learning; it's where much of your child's opinions, thoughts, and attitudes are shaped. Include your children in conferences as you see fit. These meetings can provide teachable moments on how to handle conflict and find solutions.

For example, I had a sixth-grade student (middle school) in my English Language Arts class who struggled with essays, yet this student was smart, capable, and typically excelled in all subjects. His parents continued to advocate for him as his frustrations were taken out on me. Since I was the one grading his work, it was natural for him to think I was simply a harsh grader. However, during one of our parent-teacher conferences, we went over the exact issues he didn't understand, which included creating strong thesis statements with supporting examples. Once these problems were understood, both the student and his parents realized what was missing; with all of our support, his grade improved from a "D" to a "B" in the class. More importantly, he not only learned the necessary skills to write a strong essay, he learned how to properly handle conflict and frustration.

Parent-Teacher Communication

As an educator, my advice to parents is to connect with teachers. The more information you share with teachers about your child, the easier it will be for them to modify the curriculum to meet your children's needs. Teachers desire input and help both inside and outside of the classroom; if you find that your child is struggling, please take time to connect with your child's teacher. He or she will share knowledge and information with you to help you assist your child at home. We must collaborate for student success because a strong elementary foundation is key to later growth and learning.

As an assistant principal of an elementary school, I found that even just 20 minutes a night that caregivers spent with students helped them succeed immensely in school. Those young students who did not receive much support at home often became mischievous at school, finding their way to my office to face the consequences. At school, those teachers who doted on and read books to their students helped them thrive. In fact, these students' primary language was Spanish, but with the extra love and support from their teachers, they learned English quickly. Additionally, many of those students who ran out of their classrooms in fits of frustration began staying in their classrooms, not wanting to leave their devoted teachers. Spending time with students shows them how important and appreciated they are. We all want to feel valued. These teachers valued them!

Additionally, students who connected strongly with their families, teachers, support staff, and administrators felt fulfilled and happy. These young students would enter the campus glowing with their accomplishments. When I did my rounds walking through classrooms, students would run to me, sharing what they'd learned and how they'd accomplished their assignments. Children love to do well and share their triumphs with the adults in their lives. We must allow them this opportunity and appreciate their accomplishments, no matter how big or small they may be. This is vital in nurturing strong and caring individuals.

Tips For Parenting Elementary-Aged Children:

1. See your children as they are; help with deficits and encourage their strengths.
2. Intervene when necessary, and be sure all perspectives are clear.
3. Show support by listening.
4. Create daily schedules, while allowing time for relaxation.
5. Pair secluded students with others to have lunch and other activities.
6. Provide activities in the classroom to include all students.
7. Reach out to other parents and create play dates at the park.
8. Find community leagues for sports and arts in which your children can participate.

9. Befriend school and neighborhood families to build long-lasting relationships.

10. Get involved with your school!

CHAPTER 6

MIDDLE SCHOOL

Middle school offers a very different experience for children than elementary school. The elementary world often protects and shelters young students; parents take comfort in knowing their children's teachers and the consistent support and care they provide to their kids. *So, what changes in middle school? How are the middle school years different? What does a typical middle school day look like?*

Supporting Middle School-Aged Students

In my experience, as both a parent and an educator, I've found middle school students are often faced with the following challenges:

- Anxiety surrounding feelings of loneliness, often within one's family and/or at school.
- Handling puberty/hormonal changes, both emotionally and physically.
- Peer pressure surrounding drugs, smoking, drinking, sexual activity, etc.
- Struggling with restrictions at home and fitting in with peers.
- Impact of social media on mental health and, in extreme cases, dealing with thoughts of suicide.

Teaching to the Middle School Student

Middle school teachers, and higher education teachers in general, have a passion for the subject they teach. They desire to share their knowledge and skills with students in an effort to invoke passion for certain career paths and hobbies. This differs from elementary school teachers; while there are particular subjects taught in grade school, the teacher's main focus is to teach to the student. These kids still need a lot of guidance while middle schoolers are expected to become more independent and less reliant on their teachers.

So, how do we service these middle school students? The key is for parents to retain some control. Again, just like in elementary school, creating a schedule or program for your children to follow will ensure they're making progress while obtaining the necessary skills for future growth and success.

The Middle School Day

Once students enter middle school, they no longer have a true "homeroom" and a single teacher with a permanent desk and a cubby to store their supplies. Instead, in middle school, one period is longer than the others to allow for announcements. Otherwise, students rotate to different classrooms for different subjects, carrying their backpacks with them full of books and supplies. In fact, unlike when many of us were in school, today students do not have lockers anymore. This can be a big adjustment for students.

Supporting Your Struggling Student

If your child is struggling academically, meet with each of their teachers and request weekly take-home sheets or agenda books that show accomplished work. Do not discard any work until at least midterm tests, or better yet, final exams. The completed worksheets and assignments make for great study guides for final exams. Be sure your child reviews all notes and homework daily, even if it's just for ten minutes a day. This will relieve stress when it comes time to prepare for final exams.

I also recommend providing labeled folders for children to store their work. This will make it easy for them to retrieve required work, promote healthy study habits, and maintain organization. Schoolwork has a tendency to pile up; having a second set of labeled subject folders at home is perfect to transfer completed, graded work for students to continue reviewing as a study guide. This will also help to lighten their backpack load.

My children learned great study habits and organizational skills in elementary school; however, it didn't transfer over smoothly to middle school. This is not unusual. I recall many of my middle school students following the same pattern. Typically, after the fall parent/teacher conferences in which a "game plan" was created, students found more success. Being a parent *and* a teacher gave me some unique insight both inside and outside of the classroom. Ultimately, I found academic success to be contingent on organization; and organization always begins with the student writing down the daily assignments. My children knew if they didn't write down assignments and take control of their work by midterm of the first quarter, I would request a conference with their teachers. Even when tightening the reins on my children, they still maintained control and autonomy. This is integral for their growth and success.

Of course, slip-ups can and will occur. Peer pressure and social media are some of the culprits. This is why strong reinforcements to maintain proper behavior and study habits are so essential. Sure, there will be fights, screaming, and the occasional silent treatment, that comes with the territory of parenting a teenager. In middle school, kids are really just begging for love and boundaries. If not received, chaos brews.

I won't sugarcoat it; middle school can be excruciating for children and parents alike. As a parent, I'd never felt so many emotions. It's important to remember that life for the modern middle schooler is very different than it was for their parents. While playing into the comparison game can be easy, do your best not to compare your experiences. Instead, take time to truly listen to your children's problems rather than dismissing them. If they're made to feel like their problems are not valid, children will shut down and put up barriers, preventing any further communication.

I had a student approach me and say she wished she could stay with me after school every day. She felt alone at home; she lacked self-motivation to complete her homework and her family didn't bother to encourage her. This shows how important it is to have a schedule and enforced consequences for children in middle school. While their behavior and rebellious attitude may not always show it, kids ultimately crave structure.

Supporting your child doesn't necessarily mean accepting every single decision they make or thought they share with you. But it does mean assisting them through their learning experiences and recognizing teachable moments along the way. It also includes being their cheerleader when needed and their advocate when warranted.

Impact of Parent/Teacher Communication and School Division

I taught middle school for many years, and I always embraced parental contact. I communicated through emails, phone calls, and in-person parent/teacher conferences. Furthermore, I scheduled in person meetings when warranted either from me or from the parents. Students are often motivated when they hear their teachers and parents rave about their successes. Typically, middle school teachers don't reach out to families as much, so it's up to the parent to initiate contact. These meetings offer excellent opportunities to discuss areas for improvement as well as a student's strengths. Attending conferences, calling teachers, and emailing them are all ways to model the value of your child's education.

I recall a smiling student entering my classroom the day after I had a meeting with her parents. She embraced me and shared how happy she was after the praise she'd received from her parents the previous night. They were thrilled to learn about her achievements in my class and her continued engagement, respect, and effort. This student had struggled at the beginning of the year but worked hard and, with the extra praise, she felt validated. She continued to do well and flourish in all of her classes. Simple recognition of respect, effort, and integrity goes a long way with students, just as with adults.

Another note of importance is what grades/ages define middle school; by that I mean, which grades are included in your district's middle school years. For instance, in Arizona, there are at least three different divisions of middle school. They include grades 6-8, 7-8, and 7-9. On the surface level, this may not seem like a big deal. But consider students in sixth grade; they're still young (pre-teens) and need extra nurturing. On the other hand, ninth graders

(14 year olds) are now grouped in high school with 17-18 year olds who are looking at colleges. Ninth graders are not even able to drive yet! These students should not be paired with students deemed "adults" by societal standards (18 years of age). It is critical for parents to consider these leveled boundaries when enrolling their children in school districts. The peer pressure that occurs when certain grades are mixed in one school can be overwhelming for students.

This is another reason why it's critical to have a solid relationship with your child so you can get a better sense of what he or she can cope with. Personally, I believe our schools should reframe grades so that Pre-K-6th remains elementary, 7th-9th is middle school, and 10th-12th is high school. Dividing students into these groups would help limit insecurity, peer pressure, and poor decision-making.

Tips For Parenting Middle Schoolers:

1. Implement flexible boundaries while creating an after-school checklist.

2. Ensure your children write down all the assignments for the day or week. Many schools utilize special programs such as Google Classroom to post assignments. Learn the program and review it weekly with your children.

3. Stay current with school and classroom news. Most teachers and districts provide weekly emails.

4. Ask specific questions of your children regarding school. Do not be vague. Your children might resent this, but ultimately, they will appreciate it.

5. Participate in your students' classes (many teachers incorporate long-term projects and need volunteers).

6. Meet other parents and arrange carpools.

7. Listen to your children's ideas, issues, and problems. They need to feel validated.

8. Help your child with multiple viable solutions rather than lofty ones you know they won't do (it must keep their "enthusiasm" in check).

9. Provide various schedules that students can choose from and accommodate to their lives, allowing ownership to take place.

10. Teachers should modify the topics of assignments to incorporate his/her interest.

CHAPTER 7

HIGH SCHOOL, COLLEGE, OR CAREER-BOUND

Oh boy, high school! These years are critical for your child's growth and how they will move forward in the world. With high school comes not only continued pressures from classwork, social media, and peers but also college decisions, extracurriculars, volunteer work, and more. Exhausting!

It's often said that the smaller children are, the smaller the problems and, conversely, the bigger they are, the bigger the problems. For parents, it can be difficult to watch kids grow up and face these bigger issues; we had more control of their lives when they were young, and we could offer more protection. Now, they're mini-adults with their own views and unique aspirations.

Often, students in these grades struggle with the following issues:

- Deciding whether college, technical school, or the job market is their next step.
- Anxiety about "getting into" competing institutions.
- Scoring well on ACT/SAT standardized exams.
- Feeling unsure about the future.
- Leaving home and handling problems alone.
- Conflicting feelings, desiring family but wanting to break away.

These moments are bittersweet. As the years flew by I found myself wishing it was Kindergarten my kids were entering rather than college. It's incredible to think I will miss dishes left in their rooms, socks on the floor, countless loads of laundry, crumbs everywhere, and silly arguments over curfews and other trivial affairs. Remember to cherish every moment with your kids. While it's important to teach responsibility, let the insignificant issues fall to the wayside.

Students at this age often think they know *everything,* yet they do need gentle reminders that there is still much to be learned. We must remember, no matter how much arguing may result, we are servicing them by sticking to what we know works. Getting involved at their high school, staying active, listening, and supporting them is paramount!

Guiding Children Through Adult Challenges

Conflict or disagreement with teachers is even more prevalent in high school. Our children, now young adults, know what they like and dislike. We continue to teach our children that they can learn lessons from teachers who they don't agree with, just as much as from those they adore. All of these lessons are instrumental in building a well-rounded person who can deal with the realities of life.

When my son was having difficulties in a class, he didn't become distraught. We simply figured out why certain study methods weren't working by talking to his teachers. This is what life's about. We all look for "tricks of the trade" to assist us in our tasks. My son looked at it as a process, and discovered new methods to prepare. *And guess what?* He improved! And he'll take that knowledge as he moves forward into college and beyond in the workforce.

Learning the need for a process rather than the result is critical. Unlike previous years when I had to intervene, my son is finding solutions on his own. What more can a parent (or an employer) ask for?

High school is difficult for any parent. However, this is the time we need to cut children loose and let them fend for themselves, while supporting them from afar. As they move on toward college or a career, we will not be depended on as much. Of course, we will NEVER leave our children stranded, especially in need; however, we hope they will have obtained the skills necessary to manage the daily obstacles they encounter and feel satisfied with the outcomes.

Prepping Children Through Transitions

Approaching their upperclassmen years in high school, students become more "adultish." It's funny, they begin to fault you for not teaching and ingraining in them the seriousness of school from their early years, as they now see the importance of it. As they apply to colleges, vocational schools, or work, all their inadequacies rest upon YOUR shoulders instead of THEIRS! You will be amazed at how much your children may claim that you wronged them, when you thought you did everything right! Maturity eventually surfaces with responsibility, not blaming others.

Through several experiences with my own children, I have learned that intervening sparingly has helped my children communicate better with their teachers and receive the assistance needed to succeed. For example, once again, my son has not performed as well as he wished in his chemistry class. He had a very brief, 10-minute Zoom meeting with his teacher to discuss alternative study methods. This approach further solidified their relationship and provided him tools to help him prepare/study for class. As students advance in high school, it is important to "back off" and let them figure out their path to success. However, they are still young and their brains are not fully matured. It is up to the parent to realize when to intervene in a subtle way to steer them back towards the right path.

For example, many of the high school teachers I mentored dealt with students and parents struggling to support the transition from high school to college. Parents claimed they provided as much support as possible to help their children while the students still felt unprepared. Any big transition in one's life can prove to be difficult and bring on anxiety. In *Ellevate*

Networks, "Managing Anxiety While in Transition," the author states:

> Transition is a moment in life when you're between two comfortable situations: an old and a new one. That in-between can be very uncomfortable and comes in various forms: changing a habit, facing the unknown, learning a new skill or language, joining a new company or group, moving, living in a new country, etc.

> Transition makes your stomach flip, your mouth dry, your body feel awkward or powerless and your brain functions improperly.

> Transitions are important, even though they feel unpleasant. They help us grow, learn, and most of all, adapt. If there were no transitions, we would be as stiff as a twig and we would brake at any curve. Knowing that transitions are unavoidable, what's the best way to get through them?

> One side effect of transition is anxiety. Anxiety manifests itself through nervous behaviors such as eating too much or too little, watching too much television, playing games, fidgeting, procrastination, tension, pacing back and forth, worry, uneasiness, and fear. Don't mistake anxiety and fear, as the latter is a response to an immediate threat, real or perceived. Anxiety is often a mix of emotions triggered by the expectation of a future threat.

> The problem with anxiety is that if you succumb to it, it takes over like a snowball sliding down a hill. It

grows to a point where you have no power to stop it.
It's important to control anxiety before it becomes
unwieldy.

This is just the start of the challenges students may
be facing. This includes all classroom assignments
and engagement, college, workforce, vocational
school applications, and volunteering. Applications
are nerve-racking, causing an increase in anxiety.
With anxiety comes family stress. This predicament
is NORMAL! Once applications are complete, focus
can return to school, work, and social life.

Maneuvering Forward

To maneuver through college or work applications,
print out all directions and complete each application
and assignment. Discuss the process step-by-step
with each child. Work together on calendaring
deadlines. Just like in their early years, break apart
each assignment and chunk it into simpler steps.
This ensures all requirements are met.

As our children/students advance throughout
their high school years, we MUST let them spread
their wings and manage their daily tasks on their own.
Intervene if asked or when necessary. Before suggesting
solutions, seek their thoughts and resolutions first.
Keep in mind that it is best for our children to try and
fail while under our guidance, rather than when they
leave your home. Knowing they have protection will

still keep them flourishing, while feeling safe. Failure at this young age under your roof is key.

I recall my son's gifted teacher in elementary school sharing a story with us newcomers. She had a student who excelled in elementary school and did not struggle at all. In fact, middle school and high school were also easy for this student. Unfortunately, once in college, he received his first failing grade. This student did not know how to handle this. Sadly, rather than working through it (skills he lacked as he did not need them beforehand), he decided to commit suicide. This was catastrophic; no one ever wants their child to endure such pain. We must learn to *embrace* failure as lessons for growth. Suicide is never the answer; encourage your kids to lean on others for support and ask for help when needed. There's always a solution to be found.

Empathetic Listening Throughout Next Steps

Not all kids are college-bound. Some desire to enter the workforce, some want to travel, and others hope to attend trade schools. There is a place for all of us. Supporting your children with their ambitions is critical and realizing they may not follow the "plan" you had in mind for them is fine. Again, they must know that they are loved and supported no matter what path they choose. Rather than argue, it is best to talk. Communicate about the positives and negatives of their choices, and listen to their ideas with an open mind and an open heart.

Showing love and support will help your children to discover the path that's right for them. Again, regardless of our familial similarities, every member is unique. To maintain healthy relationships with our children, we must listen, support, and share our thoughts with care and encouragement.

Having worked in many facets of education, I think it's very important to remain "present" in our children's educational lives. Children are never too grown to not desire parental approval. Even as grown-ups, we still seek approval, opinions, and advice from our parents. High school can be very difficult and challenging for students. In fact, many students "shut down" by not participating in class, failing to do homework, and not engaging in classroom conversations. It is easy for students to be swallowed up with peer pressure, both in-person and online, or they may be scared to move into the next stage of their lives. Students who continue to complete homework, projects, participate in class conversations, and are respectful tend to have the continued support of their families.

I recall a high school teacher I mentored who had a student who shut down. The student did not want to participate in class; she'd stay silent or yell out obscenities. When observing these behaviors, I asked the teacher if I could sit with the young girl in the hall for a chat. The student was incredibly reluctant, but once we eased into a conversation, I asked her how she was feeling and what she was thinking about. My questions surprised her; adults in her life usually didn't bother to ask this young girl open-ended questions. Over time, she opened up to me and it was clear her issues needed to be addressed.

She felt worthless both at home and at school. She had nowhere to go to feel important. We addressed these issues and discussed what she could do for herself. She realized, as a junior in high school, that she was in control of her own life and, thus, decided to take the "bull by its horns!" We also provided her with school counseling to support her with her family and teachers; soon, her life shifted to a more positive light.

Basically, we must do what we can to support ALL students and learn where they are AT and move them forward from there with the resources we have. It takes a *team*. Never forget it, but be ON BOARD!

Importance of Empathetic Listening

Many students feel pressured to advance their careers in a similar fashion to their family members. Advancement includes: advanced degrees, attorney, business owner, etc. Some students find pure happiness with other careers such as: interior design, carpentry, salon schooling, medical assistance, and so forth. All these careers are necessary; none should be discarded or made to feel "less than." Every person has at least one purpose. If each person can fulfill his/her purpose, he/she would be happy and feel successful. As parents and teachers, we must support their desires and allow them to feel strong and right in their decisions. The more passionate we feel about our careers, the more fulfilled we will be. In the *Museum of Purpose* article, "Purpose," the author states:

> Research shows that having a sense of purpose is good for our well-being, and **improves our resilience to stress and even our ability to think**. The founder of positive psychology, Martin Seligman, includes meaning in his PERMA model of happiness.

If a teacher does not provide weekly assignments or opportunities to assist students in organizing work, a family member must. Although parents of high schoolers should not hover, they should still show interest, ask questions, and be concerned. These are the keys to a student's success.

Tips For Parenting High Schoolers:

1. Have students write down assignments.
2. Keep a calendar/timetable of all due dates for not only academic work, but also applications and activities. The start of the year is very busy!

3. Be patient! Students in their junior/senior years begin to feel more stressed and anxious. Patience is necessary and a listening ear is a must.

4. Enroll your student in extracurricular activities, either at school or in your community.

5. Find support to help your child: tutoring with a teacher, tutoring outside school, school district online help with peers, or free programs like Khan Academy.

6. Discover your child's interests and help support them with library books, online learning, classes, or an actual teacher/coach.

7. Discuss ALL possible future ideas. In fact, research, with your child, all careers associated with their interests.

8. If they are college-bound, look at colleges that reflect their interests.

9. Find opportunities such as jobs or internships while they are in high school that correlate with their interests, so your child develops a better understanding of what is involved. For example, if interested in working with animals, find a work position that helps veterinarians, the Humane Society, or pet resorts/camps.

10. Always support any whimsical idea your child may have. Perhaps the least likely job becomes the "perfect job!"

CHAPTER 8

SCHOOLING AT HOME

We now live in a world where at-home schooling is more accessible than ever before. From online schools and learning platforms to the ability to video chat in real-time, many students today attend school virtually. Of course, students may do so for a variety of reasons. COVID-19 saw an uptick in virtual learning for most kids when classrooms were off limits. Many families found the virtual option to better meet their needs and have continued it past the point it was mandated by public health requirements.

While virtual schooling is a boon for many families, expecting children to move through 5-7 subjects a day on their own and without the support of a live, physical teacher is unrealistic. Therefore, it is important to create a schedule to assist your child in working through each mandatory subject in a system that will help them thrive.

Catering to the Needs of Your At-Home Student

As a Home Instruction Specialist working with students who stayed home due to medical needs, I created solutions, or game plans, to assist them in learning the curriculum without feeling overwhelmed and defeated. In the Appendix section of this book, you will find templates of different ideas/strategies to implement at home to help your child move toward graduation in a successful manner.

I had one student in particular who would not leave his bed. He hid under his covers, even during online instructional one-on-one time with a teacher. To combat this, I had many conversations with the teacher, parent, and student to discuss what we needed to do to engage him. Our solution was to only work on one or two subjects a day, and in very small doses. Every couple of weeks, we were able to increase the amount of instructional time. Homework was limited, but he did participate more as the weeks progressed.

The point is, it can be very challenging to motivate students who are being schooled from home. Anxiety and other mental health issues make it even more challenging. It is crucial to begin your work where the student is, and slowly increase the amount and complexity of the work as they can handle it. It's like any other activity; you have to build up bit by bit rather than attacking it all at once.

Strategies to Optimize At-Home Schooling:

A. Take Breaks!

Whether or not your child attends school in-person, breaks are crucial. Imagine working a full-time job with absolutely no breaks in the day. *Could you sit at your desk job without any breaks? Do you have any desire to chat with coworkers about anything other than your responsibilities or supervisors?* We are all people– and people crave connections! We need rest and conversations with others who understand us. Our children are just like us– they need this too!

There are positives and negatives to home-schooling. Positives include seeing your children more, less distraction from peers, and more parental control. However, home-schooled students lose out on social time, peer and teacher thoughts and revelations, and interaction with others. If home-schooling or online schooling is the choice you made, think carefully about enrolling your child in extra-curricular activities. Children must have social interactions to become well-rounded adults.

According to the Coalition for Responsible Home Education:

> Your child needs unscripted access to peers; privacy as they build and maintain friendships; and frequent interaction with friends and other peers. While every child's needs differ, in general, your child needs access to non-sibling peers, with time and space to interact, multiple times per week (if not daily). Homeschooled children's contact with peers may take a variety of forms,

including co-ops, classes, clubs, children's programming, and playdates.

B. Food and Exercise

Research has shown that our population has gained weight during the COVID-19 pandemic. Much of this is due to the immense amount of unstructured time spent at home, sitting more, and gathering stockpiles of food in the pantry and fridge since dining in restaurants was forbidden. According to PAN American Journal of Health (PAHO):

> These changes can be associated with two important aspects. First, staying at home, which includes working remotely, studying, or spending many hours per day in front of a computer, with little outdoor physical activity. Second, the storage of food at home due to the existing restrictions to go outside to purchase food. In addition, the interruption of the work routine caused by quarantine could result in boredom, which in turn might be associated with an increased caloric intake.

> Unfortunately, these behaviors are difficult to break. Returning to a brick and mortar school building and the workplace has helped many return to a healthier lifestyle.

For those families with children still schooling from home, it is beneficial to make changes that will enable the above behaviors to stop and incorporate healthier choices. For example, stock the refrigerator with healthy food options such as fruits, vegetables, and whole grains. Find healthier alternatives for pantry items.

According to Dr. Wolfe's *A Diet is the Last Thing You Need*, an eating schedule is an excellent way to circumvent overindulging. Dr. Wolfe states:

...it is best to have a generally regular schedule of when you eat. In fact, scheduling food intake every two to four hours will prevent you from becoming so hungry that you lose control when you do eat. For most people that roughly means breakfast, lunch, and dinner, with a snack between at least two of them (p. 137-138).

Create a daily schedule that incorporates exercise time. Be sure to include at least 60 minutes of cardiovascular exercise. The 60 minutes does not have to occur all at once, but instead may be spread out throughout the day. According to Centers for Disease Control and Prevention:

Recommendations for Children and Adolescents Ages 6 Through 17 Years 60 minutes or more of moderate-to-vigorous intensity physical activity each day.

- Aerobic activity: Most of the daily 60 minutes should include activities like walking, running, or anything that makes their hearts beat faster. At least 3 days a week should include vigorous-intensity activities.
- Muscle-strengthening: Includes activities like climbing or doing push-ups, at least 3 days per week.
- Bone-strengthening: Includes activities such as jumping or running, at least 3 days per week.

In fact, the CDC's article, "Moving Matters for My Health," reinforces that activities can be spread out throughout the week and even the day.

Some activities are better than none! Adults need at least 150 minutes a week of moderate-intensity activity. That might sound like a lot, but you can spread your activity out during the week. For example, you could do 22 minutes of physical activity every day or 30 minutes 5 days a week. You can also count smaller chunks of physical activity during the day, like 5 minutes of climbing stairs.

C. Foster a Social Life

Human beings need to feel worthwhile. They need to have a purpose and feel connected to others and a greater good. In fact, research shows that human beings need to have some form of "touching," such as a hug, to feel content. We *crave* these connections. According to PsychCentral, relationships with others can decrease depression, increase happiness, provide better stability in mood management, create a longer lifespan and quality of life, and increase personal fulfillment. In their article, "The Importance of Connection," it states:

> Human connection is the sense of closeness and belongingness a person can experience when having supportive relationships with those around them. Connection is when two or more people interact with each other and each person feels valued, seen, and heard. There's no judgment, and you feel stronger and nourished after engaging with them. Human connection can be a chat over coffee with a friend, a hug from a partner after a long day, or a hike in the woods with a family member.

Every human being needs peer interaction. If schooling and/or working from home, it is imperative to enroll your child in activities that can provide connections with others. Of course, visiting with family and neighborhood friends is wonderful, but peer interaction is necessary. Additionally, children need to explore their interests outside academics. It is important that they pursue their interests whether it is sports, crafts, cooking, gardening, music, or specialized clubs. Students can enroll in after-school activities at their homebound school. Additionally, cities have Parks and Recreation programs that cater to various age groups. Suggest and provide ideas to help your child explore these opportunities and take part.

If we want our children to grow into well-rounded adults, they must have a balanced lifestyle. A balanced lifestyle includes school, activities (individual and with peers), family, healthy eating, exercise, and much love.

CHAPTER 9

SPECIAL MOMENTS

Being a parent is time-consuming and difficult. However, it is also a loving, rewarding, and an amazing experience. Children crave love and boundaries. Below are some suggestions to continue fostering special moments with your children through their schooling years and beyond.

School Video Clips

Many families share pictures of their children on the first day of each new school year. Go a step beyond and video record your children's hopes and dreams for that new school year and then record them on their last day as well. Let them reflect on their highlights of the year. These recordings not only provide pictures but provide you their voice, behaviors, mannerisms, and aspirations as well!

Cook-Ins v. Eat Outs

For most children, going out to dinner is FUN! However, I found that turning the tables around and creating our own meals from scratch at home can be just as enjoyable. Therefore, during my children's high school years, we implemented Sunday night "Cook-Ins." We collected recipes, and our children chose a recipe to make Sunday nights. The purpose is to teach them how to cook so that when they leave the house, they are equipped to maintain hearty, healthy meals.

Cooking Competition/Decorating Competition

Along with the above idea, my family also teamed up (two v. two) and cooked recipes or created crafts as a competition. It's not about which team is better, but more about the fun and laughter that came about during the process. This has brought many moments of joy and laughter within our family, not to mention delicious meals. We also played around with crafts, allowing for many fun holiday moments: Halloween, Thanksgiving, Valentine's Day, 4th of July, and beyond.

Game Night

We have loved playing board games since our children were little. We had so much fun playing Chutes and Ladders, Sorry, Candyland, Gin Rummy, Connect Four, Memory cards, to name a few. As our children aged and COVID arrived, we turned our fun family game nights into friendly games of competition. We created a list of rewards, such as picking out our next family movie, dinner option, event and such. Our games expanded to UNO, Monopoly, Risk, and others. These nights are so fun and engaging, that even their friends joined in! Anytime we are able to incorporate face-time with our children (screens left behind), our nights become positively filling.

Movie Night

Our family loves movies. Most Sunday nights, a different family member chooses a movie to watch. After cooking our food, we gather in the family room and watch a movie together. Although one chooses the movie, we all tend to narrow the field to a few we would all enjoy and then the lucky person chooses. This is a fun and relaxing way to end the weekend. We all wind down eating, laughing, and enjoying ourselves before the new week begins.

Puzzles

Another great family activity is doing puzzles! Working on puzzles allows for a lengthy stretch of time together. In fact, we tend to do it all together and separately. We are a family of four, so sometimes two or three of us work on it at a time. It is an experience that allows for frustration and elation to occur. Frustration is important, as it teaches our children to learn patience and understand that situations can and will be difficult at times, but the willingness to persevere through these moments is critical. Not only do puzzles teach patience, but they also teach children to think logically. Logic is another vital skill children need to embrace.

Gardening

Planting and tending to beautiful flowers not only creates a lovely environment but also provides a feeling of accomplishment. Look for seasonal flowers so they last longer! Building a garden is a great way to teach your kids about responsibility as well. Additionally, growing a vegetable garden not only has the same impact, but contributes to healthy eating. My family enjoys cooking with the fresh produce we harvest from our own garden. Growing vegetables takes some preparation but is highly rewarding. Be sure to research which vegetables grow best in each season where you live. Currently in our Arizona-based garden we are growing eggplants, peppers, tomatoes, zucchini, broccoli, kale, chard, and herbs! Including these items during our Sunday night "Cook-Ins" is fun and enjoyable.

Karaoke/Online Game Night

Singing and competing on gaming devices such as Playstation is a fun and highly engaging activity to do as a family and with family friends in person or online. For years we have enjoyed participating in this activity. Many times we would have early meals while belting out the latest songs on our Karaoke machine. This is a great activity for long weekends, rainy nights, and whenever all are in the mood! Competing, winning, and losing are all valuable skills our children must learn to deal with. Children must learn to be gracious winners and not sore losers. To ease this lesson, we played on teams. Children learned how to cope with both winning and losing, and we were able to compete solo. This is true with board games as well. Children need baby steps. There are so many valuable teachable moments within "fun time."

One-on-One Vacations/Moments

Although we enjoy family vacations, my husband and I realized the necessity that each of our children needs some one-on-one time. We decided that each year, we (one of us with one child) would take a child on a vacation for the weekend. These moments have been incredibly precious, beautiful, and memorable. The same valuable experience can be had with just taking a neighborhood walk, swimming together, or playing a game. The key is to provide your child with undivided attention. I strongly recommend taking moments to spend with one child at a time. Many ideas include: a walk, swim, vacation, hike, run, see a movie, shop, go to a restaurant, partake in arts and crafts projects, or cook together. Choose something weekly or even monthly. This is a time that will be remembered and cherished forever.

Mementos

1. Personalized objects or a collage: blankets, mugs, containers personalized with your child's photo or biographic details. Parent/child symbolic jewelry.

2. A stream of video clips from the first to last day of each school year.

3. A family picture collage that showcases life events throughout the years.

Takeaway

We have covered a lot of topics and discussed many strategies throughout the pages of this book. My hope is that most, if not all, of it will be useful to you as you navigate the exciting journey that is child-rearing. However, throughout your journey, the most important message I hope you take away is this: All children, like all people, want to be heard, understood, and valued. Communicate with your family with an empathetic ear, and an open mind and heart. Love and openness allow wounds to heal and children to flourish.

CHAPTER 10

APPENDIX

Appendix 1- Most Common Challenges by Age Range:

There is considerable variability between school districts with respect to the distribution of grades between elementary, middle, and high-school. Nonetheless, the needs of your child at each age-span remain the same. The following chart itemizes the most common challenges children experience within different age ranges. Regardless of what particular grade your child is in, being aware of his or her emotional development will help you most effectively help her/him navigate the period.

Grades K-5 (6 or 7)	Grades 6-7 (7-9)	Grades 9-12 (10-12)
Anxiety among friends and teachers.	Anxiety among peers and speaking out in front of the class.	Anxiety competing for colleges, career path, and social life balanced with GPA.
Lack of structure.	Puberty and emotional issues.	SAT/ACT and other testing to influence the future.
Hard time grasping material.	Handling pressures to use drugs/ alcohol/ tobacco, stealing.	Feeling alone by not having a game plan for the future like peers.
Not feeling appreciated by teachers.	Being called upon to approach the whiteboard when not able to (hormonal issues for both genders).	Uncertainty leaving home- excited but nervous.

Grades K-5 (6 or 7)	Grades 6-7 (7-9)	Grades 9-12 (10-12)
Lonely and ostracized by peers.	Friction with parents-needing approval but pulling away.	Too young to see how the future will unfold and not sure which "decision" to make.
Lack of fundamental skills (reading/math).	Suicide news/media and actual reality.	Pressure from parents, teachers, and peers.
Not being selected to join a PE team for a sport.	Not feeling valued or wanted.	Not feeling valued or wanted.
Not feeling valued or wanted.	Distinguishing between belonging in a group and disappointing parents.	Distinguishing between belonging in a group and disappointing parents.

Appendix 2- Study Schedule:

Attending School and After School Hours- create a plan to follow for the "in between hours" of school and evening. Schedules aid in concentration, fulfillment, and success. This is one area that should be addressed weekly.

- At home, eat a healthy snack and relax. Socialize with family and friends for 15 minutes.

- Look at the assignment book or online for all required homework.

- Calendar work in priorities: do immediate work and calendar long-term projects, providing enough time each day by breaking down projects into attainable chunks to complete the project on time.

- Once immediate work is completed, take a 10-20 minute break (depending on after school activities). If not involved in sports, take the time to exercise and then begin portions of any long-term projects. If there are no long-term projects, take the time to review your work and study for quizzes and tests.

- Spend the afternoon with your activities or more exercise. Before or after dinner, review for any quizzes/tests again.

- Enjoy the rest of the evening.

Schooling at Home-Schedules to support children's education, activities, and health.

- Wake up following a normal school schedule (breakfast, brush teeth, stretch, check phone messages)... perhaps 7:00 a.m.

- Eat a healthy breakfast and then exercise for at least 20 minutes or reverse it. Some people prefer eating before exercise and some the opposite.

- Look at your classes and write down all required assignments for the day and those due the following day (as this occurs daily, it is only ensuring you are on target).

- Calendar any long-term projects and portion the work out into chunks assigning a portion per day.

- Spend one-two hours (depending on age) working. Begin with the easiest work and file it away in an organized fashion (organization is addressed in Appendices 5 and 6).

- Take a 15 minute break to walk or bike outside. Enjoy your neighborhood, your backyard, or a nearby park.

- Spend another hour or two (depending on age) continuing to work on your assignments/ classes.

- Again, take another 15-20 minute break. Maybe take a walk while talking to friends on the phone, listening to music, or playing online games.

- Enjoy a healthy snack (See Appendix 3 for healthy snack suggestions).

- Return to work and continue following this process until all work is completed.

- Enjoy your lunch and an activity (assume an hour break).

- Continue working on what is leftover or review work to prepare for quizzes and tests.

- Take a 20 minute break outdoors.

- Review everything once again and ensure all materials are ready for the next day and the rest of the week.

- Dinner.

- Enjoy the evening.

Appendix 3- Snack Alternatives:

Healthy alternatives, especially with boredom and depression will help maintain focus and energy. It is easy to grab the simplest and unhealthiest item. However, if we take time to provide reasonable healthier alternatives, our children will feel better and do better.

- Always prepare snacks for the week on the weekend so they are ready to eat when hungry.

- Air fry or bake sweet potatoes, beets, asparagus, zucchini (really anything), lightly salting them (great substitute for chips).

- Protein bars such as Clif bars, Power Crunch, and the Zone bar (there are many more) are all healthier alternatives than candy bars.

- Dip apples or bananas into honey or add a little Swerve sweetener.

- Find recipes to freeze bananas and then mash them to create a type of ice cream... fresh strawberries and blueberries can be added to them. There are many frozen fruit/ice cream recipes online.

- Nuts, but in small doses. If buying a bag, separate them into small snack bags that can become a "grab and go" bag. This will help deter the desire for chips or cookies.

- Add a scoop of peanut butter to apples or bananas. If they have a sore throat, substitute the peanut butter for some Agave honey.

- Whole grain toast with avocado or peanut butter. This is very filling. Even a drizzle of cheese on bread with avocado can make this appetizing. Don't do too much of anything; just add enough to satisfy the hunger and craving.

- Hummus with celery, carrots, and whole grain chip options. Avocado dip is also something that can easily be made and is a healthy dip for veggies and chips.

- Greek yogurt with fresh fruit and/or healthy granola mixed in. This is very filling and healthy.
- Trail mix- Mix the following into a snack bag: raisins, almonds, cashews, Brazil nuts, Macadamia nuts, dark chocolate, banana chips, and cranberries.
- Drink PLENTY of water throughout the day. We often think we are hungry, but really, we are dehydrated. Be sure to always drink water before, during, and after you eat. You will be surprised with how much less food you consume.

Appendix 4- Exercise:

Exercise at home to maintain fitness, health, and mindfulness. All of the following exercise ideas can be completed in the luxury of your own home. You DO NOT have to join a gym. Exercising three to four times a day for just ten minutes each time will maintain your energy and health throughout the day.

- Long, fast-paced walks
- Running
- Bicycling
- Jumping jacks/jump rope
- Abdominal exercises and push ups

- We instituted at home: 30-30-30. Throughout the day, we do 30 jumping jacks, 30 abdominal crunches, and 30 push-ups
- 5-10 minute program

We instituted 5-10 minutes of an afternoon workout that incorporated:

- Climbing stairs- 5 times
- Jumping jacks- 30 times
- Burpees- 10 times
- Push-ups- 10 times
- Mountain climbers- 10 times

Every day we focused on different exercises; typically a total of three. You can find more ideas online/apps.

Appendix 5- After-School Schedule to Support Goal Accomplishment:

- Prioritize your homework immediately and create a weekly schedule that will ensure you complete your homework on time.
- Create a calendar that timelines sports/activities events, homework, and project due dates.
- Be sure to list when each task should be completed, and stick to it.

- Have ready-made, proportional healthy snacks available. Eat periodically with a lot of water.

- If none of your after-school programs include physical activity, incorporate breaks that include 10-15 minute intervals.

- Exercise will help you be alert, feel good, and focus on your studies and activities.

- Incorporate 30/30/30 (30 push-ups, 30 sit-ups, 30 jumping jacks).

  This can be repeated throughout the day. In fact, this can be broken down within one round of 10:10:10 repeated three times. The point is, this is beneficial for anyone, can be completed anywhere, provides exercise health, and allows one to get back to work without having to shower and change. It is a quick break that should take about three minutes.

Appendix 6- Organizational Skills to Stay on Task and Reach Academic and Nonacademic Goals:

- If not provided an agenda book from school, create your own calendar or buy one.

- List all assignments in it.

- Break down long-term projects (more common in upper grades) and create soft due dates to ensure every integral portion is completed without feeling stressed.

- Create an after school schedule that allows relaxation, but also allows enough time for homework and activities.

Appendix 7- Learning Games:

To understand academic material in a fun, less anxious environment:

There are many online games to help students learn course material. Examples include Kahoot It! and Quizlet. There are also applications that help with learning states and capitals, phonics, math, and more. Additionally, programs such as IXL and Khan Academy are also excellent for teaching or learning new skills.

When reviewing for tests in my household, we would turn the material into songs or rhymes. For example, when learning all the bones in the body, we would create gestures and sounds that would not just provide a clue to what they represent but were memorable.

Just by spending time with your children reviewing and turning it into a game, such as making memory cards (remember the memory card game), learning can be enjoyable, helpful, and allow for bonding together.

Appendix 8- Sentence Starters for Difficult Conversations:

These sentence starters will assist you in maintaining positive conversation with your children and understanding the root of it. These are provided by pnwboffice.com.

- I agree with you because...
- I learned that....
- Could you please tell me about...
- I noticed that...
- Could you explain your answer?
- I understand what you are saying, but I think...
- May I suggest something?
- May I point out...
- This makes me think about....
- This reminds me of...
- What I heard you say...
- I'm surprised that...
- According to the text...
- This makes me wonder about...
- Help me understand...
- I figured out that...
- I think you (or someone) is trying to say....
- Could you show me/explain to me...

Appendix 9- Shifting Your Thinking:

Ideas received from, *Communication Starters: According to Scholastic Inc:* "Conversation Starters Bulletin Act."

Change From...	To.....
I stink at this!	How can I improve?
I give up/I'm so frustrated.	Is there another way to approach this? Maybe there is a different method or strategy I can utilize.
I'm so dumb; I'm not smart like others.	I will learn this until I understand it!
It's fine....it's good enough...it doesn't matter.	Can I do better?
It's impossible!	I'm going to do my best!
It is awful; I give up!	How can I improve it?
I made a mistake/I'm going to fail.	Failure is a lesson; I will do my best and learn from my mistakes for next time.

Appendix 10- Tutoring Support from the Author:

Sessions are affordable and provide available strategies to maintain extra support for the following:

- Organizational skills
- Study skills
- Scheduling/Calendaring
- Tutoring in each subject (as many per hour that can be accomplished)
- Social-emotional support
- Reviewing material
- Learning social skills (with peers and adults)
- Editing work: for example, research reports, essays, various writings (entrance essays, resumes, etc.)

Offering virtual and in-person sessions. Please contact the author at:

Corinne Forman, M.Ed.
www.seedingroots.com
support@seedingroots.com

WORKS CITED

"10 Ways to Help Your Teen Succeed in High School (for Parents) - Nemours Kidshealth." Edited by Kathryn Hoffses, KidsHealth, The Nemours Foundation, Aug. 2018, https://kidshealth.org/en/parents/school-help-teens.html.

"Ashley Growth Mindset Magnetic Mini BBS, 12' X 17' (ASAH77010): Staples." Staples.com, https://www.staples.com/Ashley-Growth-Mindset-Magnetic-Mini-BBS-12-x-17-ASAH7710/product_24063296.

Bisnow, Margot Machol, and Contributor. "I Talked to 70 Parents Who Raised Highly Successful Adults-Here's the 'Rare' Skill They All Taught Their Kids." CNBC, CNBC, 7 Nov. 2022, https://www.cnbc.com/2022/11/05/i-talked-to-70-parents-who-raised-highly-successful-adults heres-the-rare-skill-they-all-taught-their-kids.html.

"Checking Your Browser before Accessing Www.pnwboffice. com." - PNWB Office Products, https://www. pnwboffice.com/Products/Conversation-Starters- -Bulletin-Board-Set---Oder-of-1-Each__SC- 823624.aspx?pid=8efe7a78-a3ec-4b33-b0ae- 2baacea21a58&gclid=CoKCQiAyMKbBhD1AR IsANs7rEErebwAXxg3uJAY6Qgd1nvHhynS6 3JYeYv5FFk4wdNKha8o8VRcrgaAlCnEALw_ wcB&onatalp=1148082495&fph=0_522291b2 75034166e9add0d46cef526&mxxh=20.

"Coalition for Responsible Home Education." Coalition for Responsible Home Education, https:// responsiblehomeschooling.org/.

Dh, Mhc@. "How Does Family Life Affect Mental Health?" Mental Health Center, 8 June 2017, https://www. mentalhealthcenter.org/how-does-family- life-affect-mental-health/.

"Effort Is Virtuous: Teacher Preferences of Pupil Effort, Ability and Grading in Physical Education." Taylor & Francis, https://www.tandfonline. com/doi/abs/10.1080/0013188970390310.

Fabian, Renee. "The Psychology behind Success and Failure." Talkspace, 16 Aug. 2021,' https://www. talkspace.com/blog/psychology-behind- success-failure/.

Ferlazzo, Larry. "Advice for New Middle School Teachers from Four Veterans (Opinion)." Education Week, Education Week, 24 Jan. 2022, https://www.edweek.org/teaching-learning/opinion-middle-school-teachers-do-you-eed-advice-check-out-this-wisdom/2022/01.

Ginott, Haim G., et al. Between Parent and Child: The Bestselling Classic That Revolutionized Parent-Child Communication. Three Rivers Press, 2003.

"History of Education: The United States in a Nutshell." History of Education in the United States Educational Tools | LiM, https://www.leaderinme.org/blog/history-of-education-the-united-states-in-a-nutshel/.

History and Evolution of Public Education in the US - Eric. https://files.eric.ed.gov/fulltext/ED606970.pdf. https://www.museumofhappiness.org/news/purpose-happiness#:~:text=Research%20shows 20that%2 having%20a,his%20PERMA%20model %20of%20happiness.

Johnson, Brittani. "Digital Footprint 101: What Is a Digital Footprint & How to Protect It." Iris Powered by Generali, Apr. 2022, https://www.irisidentityprotection.com/blog/digital-footprint-101?utm_term=&utm_campaign=Dynamic%2B Search&utm_source=adwords&utm_medium=

ppc&hsa_tgt=dsa-19959388920&hsa_grp=
113023862570&hsa_mt=&hsa_cam=12352612
499&hsa_ver=3&hsa_src=g&hsa_net=adwords
&hsa_kw=&hsa_acc=5355848132&hsa_
ad=582414782790&gclid=CjoKCQjwyt-ZBh
CNARIsAKH11767wC2y1LCo1RXFZNpmkn
6fqTtENMSPJ5UTHe-5fjyqorg5Ku_x_
agaAuAvEALw_wcB.

Kuhfeld, Megan, et al. "The Pandemic Has Had
Devastating Impacts on Learning. What
Will It Take to Help Students Catch up?"
Brookings, Brookings, 3 Mar. 2022, https://
www.brookings.edu/blog/brown-center-
chalkboard/2022/03/03/the-pandemic-has
had-devastating-impacts-on-learning-what-
will-it-take-to-help-students-catch-up/#:~:tex
=In%20addition%20to%20surging%20
COVID,quarantines%2C%20and%20
rolling%20shool%20closures.

Monroe, Jamison. "The Latest on Teen Cell Phone
Addiction." Newport Academy, Newport Academy,
6 Oct. 2022, https://www.newportacademy.
com/resources/mental-health/teen-cell-
phone-addiction/?utm_source=google&utm_
medium=cpc&utm_campaign=NA_leads_
performancemax&utm_term=&kpid=go_cmp-
17884784088_adg-_ad-__dev-c_ext-_prd-
&gclid=CjoKCQjwnbmaBhD-ARIsAGTPcfXwAl

WLxlpmVQRhsRe6Do5poUNt-kincRHOFHeS1 BG74hExYRx7u98aAgVsEALw_wcB.

"Organizational Success: Factors & Definition." *Study. com*, 4 January 2016, study.com/academy/ lesson/organizational-success-factors- definition-quiz.html

"Preventing Cyberbullying." Delete Cyberbullying, https://www.endcyberbullying.net/ preventing-cyberbullying.

Russell, Dr. Lucy. "Flexible Parenting and Boundaries." *They Are the Future*, 23 July 2022, https://www. theyarethefuture.co.uk/flexible-parenting- boundaries/.

Sara Bigwood Founder. "Managing Anxiety While in Transition." Ellevate, Ellevate, 16 Dec. 2016, https://www.ellevatenetwork.com/articles/ 6571-managing-anxiety-while-in-transition.

Scholastic Inc.. Colors and Shapes Bulletin Board Set Lowes.com. https://www.lowes.com/pd/ Scholastic-Inc-Colors-and-Shapes-Bulletin- Board-Set/5001146017.

Sherrell, Zia. "School Anxiety: Causes, Symptoms, and Management." Medical News Today, MediLexicon International, 29 June 2022, https://www.medicalnewstoday.com/articles/

school-anxiety#:~:text=School%20anxiety 20is%20a%20condition,in%20public%2C%20 or%20taking%20tests.

Stiles, Katie. "Human Connection: Why It's Important." Psych Central, Psych Central, 15 Nov. 2021, https://psychcentral.com/lib/the-importance- of-connection#what-is-it.

The Children's Hospital of Philadelphia. "The Benefits of Outdoor Play: Why It Matters." Children's Hospital of Philadelphia, The Children's Hospital of Philadelphia, 3 Oct. 2019, https://www.chop. edu/news/health-tip/benefits-outdoor-play- why-it-matters#:~:text=Unstructured%20 physical%20activity%20improves%20 the,a%20result%20of%20physical%20activity.

Van Der Helden, Jurjen, et al. "Importance of Failure: Feedback-Related Negativity Predicts Motor Learning Efficiency." OUP Academic, Oxford University Press, 19 Oct. 2009, https://academic. oup.com/cercor/article/20/7/1596/322202.

Webfx. "Helping Your Child Explore Their Own Interests." Bricks 4 Kidz Kids Franchise, 12 Aug.2020, https://www.bricks4kidz.com/blog/helping- your-child-explore-their-own- interests/#:~:text=When%20children%20 are%20encouraged%20to,short%2D%20 and%20long%2Dterm.

"Weight Gain and Physical Inactivity during the COVID-19 Pandemic." Pan American Journal of Public Health, Pan American Journal of Public Health, https://www.paho.org/journal/en/articles/weight-gain-and-physical-inactivity-during-covid-19-pandemic.

"Why Do We Need to Feel Valued?" Psychology Today, Sussex Publishers, https://www.psychologytoday.com/us/blog/the-i-m-approach/202005/why-do-we-need-feel-valued.

Wolfe, Brenda L. A Diet Is the Last Thing You Need: Weight Loss and Maintenance Answers. 2021.

BIOGRAPHY

Corinne Forman is an innovative and adaptable leader whose unconventional thinking and novel ideas offer inventive solutions for today's education challenges. Differentiated by a unique combination of insightful work experience not only in public education, but also in the private sector with entrepreneurial experience in e-learning and technology development, she has over 25 years dedicated to advancing public education as an administrator, teacher mentor, teacher, entrepreneur, and community member. Corinne holds a Masters of Leadership and an administrator's certificate, as well as certificates in elementary and secondary education. Purposeful and persistent about leading in a meaningful and efficient way, she embraces collaboration and effective communication to drive her commitment in empowering educators and students alike.

Corinne has two high school-aged children, experiencing all the challenges that come along with parenthood. From peer pressure and supporting extra needs/gifted children to physical challenges, and much more, she has a wealth of diverse experiences which she desires to share in an effort to help others thrive in parenthood.

THANK YOU FOR READING.
PLEASE LEAVE A REVIEW

I hope you have enjoyed reading this book and gained some insights that can help you and your family flourish. If you think this book was valuable to you and would also benefit others, please feel free to leave a review so others are able to find this book and benefit from it.

www.ingramcontent.com/pod-product-compliance
Lightning Source LLC
Chambersburg PA
CBHW021129020426
42331CB00005B/690